AFTER THE SPILL

The Exxon Valdez Disaster Then and Now

Sandra Markle

More than 11 million gallons of gooey black oil poured into the sea—enough to fill about fourteen Olympic-sized swimming pools. The greasy oil that poured out of the Exxon Valdez *floated to the surface, then washed ashore, coating 2,490 kilometers (1,548 miles) of shoreline. The gray areas in the picture on page 3 are oil-covered land.*

What Happened Here?

Imagine the mess if you punched a can opener into the bottom of an aluminum can full of soda. Now, imagine ripping a hole in the bottom of a ship full of oil—a ship that's longer than three football fields and extends down into the water as far as an upside-down five-story building.

That's what happened just seconds after midnight on March 24, 1989. Crossing Prince William Sound to the Pacific Ocean, the crewman on duty spotted ice ahead and turned the *Exxon Valdez* out of the ship's normal route. Too big to turn easily, the ship went far off course and struck Bligh Reef, a jumble of jagged boulders just twelve meters (forty feet) below the water's surface. The rocks ripped open the ship's metal hull.

What happened next was a disaster. Cleaning up the mess cost several billion dollars and has taken years.

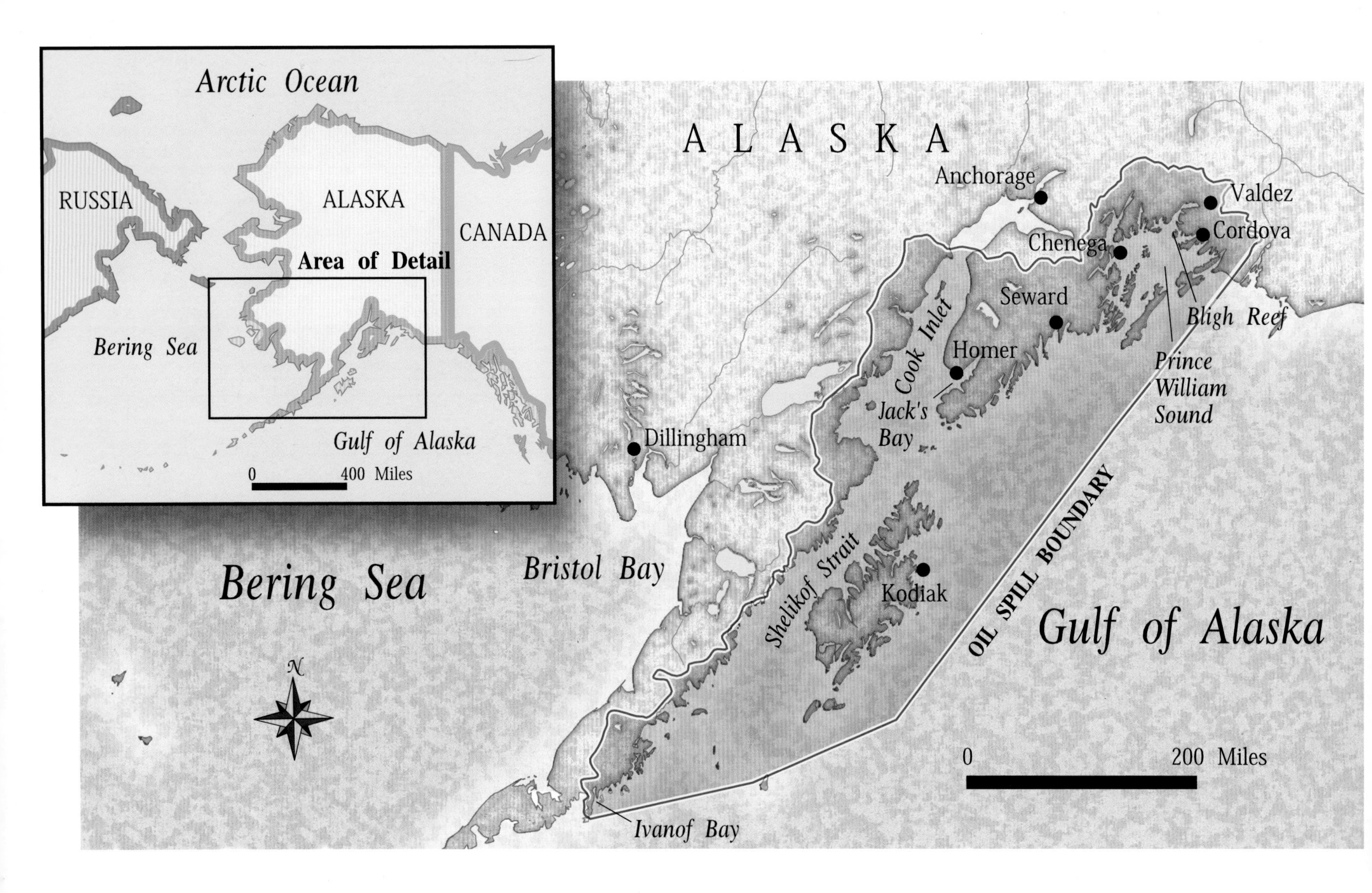
Arctic Ocean
RUSSIA
ALASKA
CANADA
Area of Detail
Bering Sea
Gulf of Alaska
0
400 Miles
ALASKA
Anchorage
Valdez
Cordova
Chenega
Seward
Bligh Reef
Cook Inlet
Homer
Prince William Sound
Jack's Bay
Dillingham
OIL SPILL BOUNDARY
Shelikof Strait
Kodiak
Bering Sea
Bristol Bay
Gulf of Alaska
N
0
200 Miles
Ivanof Bay

Why Was This Spill Such a Big Problem?

Aleyska, the company responsible for transporting the oil, was called within minutes of the wreck, but the spill took everyone by surprise. Nobody had thought such a big oil spill would ever happen, so Aleyska was caught unprepared. Although workers at Aleyska knew how to handle an ordinary spill, there weren't enough resources to clean up after the *Exxon Valdez*.

Besides being large, the *Exxon Valdez* spill was difficult to clean because of its remote location. The only way to reach the spill was by helicopter or boat.

Because the weather was clear and the sea was very calm, Aleyska officials thought the oil would just stay pooled around the shipwreck. For three days, the company's spill experts tested different plans to find the best way to clean up the spill. Then something unexpected happened. A fierce storm with high winds created strong waves that pushed the oil away from the wreck and onto the beaches. Now the mess was a disaster.

What Happened to the Animals?

This bird didn't expect oil to be floating on the water when it landed on the waves in search of a fish dinner. Its feathers immediately became coated with the oil, which let cold water reach the bird's skin. When the bird tried to clean its feathers by pulling them through its mouth, it was poisoned by swallowing the toxic oil. Many seabirds, such as cormorants and scoters, died from getting too cold or swallowing the oil.

Volunteers picked up and cleaned as many of the birds as they could, but it was a difficult process. An oily bird had to be dunked in warm soapy water while the feathers were scrubbed with a toothbrush to loosen the sticky oil. Then the soap had to be rinsed away. Usually the whole process needed to be repeated a second time. Sadly, this cleaning was stressful for the birds, and many of those that were rescued died in the process.

A bird's feathers are usually light and fluffy—perfect for trapping warm air next to the bird's skin. Coated with oil, the feathers make the bird as uncomfortable as you would be if you went outdoors to play in the snow in wet clothes.

Sea otters were victims of the *Exxon Valdez* oil spill too. When an otter swam into the oil or popped up through the slick to take a breath of air, it became coated with the sticky black stuff. Just like seabirds, sea otters depend on their fluffy coat to stay warm. Their fur traps air warmed by their body heat close to their skin. Matted with oil, the fur can no longer do its job. Naturally, the oil-coated otters tried to clean themselves the only way they knew how: by licking their fur. So they too were poisoned by swallowing the toxic oil.

Picking up oiled otters, cleaning them, and moving them to unoiled beaches took a lot of time, effort, and money. Experts at Exxon estimated that it cost about $80,000 each to rescue and clean the sea otters. Kathy Frost, of the Alaska Department of Fish and Game, reported that, sadly, many of the cleaned otters died anyway.

After they were cleaned up, sea otters were moved away from the spill area. Most of the cleaned sea otters were taken to Jack's Bay opposite Homer, Alaska, and set free.

According to the *Exxon Valdez* Oil Spill Trustee Council, the oil spill affected Alaska's pink salmon and sockeye salmon populations differently. Pink salmon leave the sea and swim up shallow streams to lay their eggs in the gravel. Waves pushed the oil up these streams, coating the pink salmon eggs. The oil killed the unborn baby salmon, greatly reducing the population of future pink salmon.

Unlike pink salmon, sockeye salmon swim way upstream and lay their eggs in lakes, so they were not affected by the spilled oil. However, since all salmon fishing was stopped the year after the spill, more adults than usual made it upstream to lay their eggs. The number of baby sockeye salmon that hatched was so large, their habitat became overcrowded. Many young sockeye salmon died because there was not enough food to feed all the hungry fish.

Pink salmon spawning at Prince William Sound.

The herring population suffered too. Because herring eggs float at the water's surface, they were coated by the oil. The year of the spill, the number of herring that hatched was much lower than normal.

Problems with the fish populations after the spill meant problems for the seabirds and sea otters that eat the fish. People were hurt too—especially those who depend on the herring fishing industry. Three years after the spill, the number of adult herring dropped so low it became hard for people to catch enough to make a living. Also, the fish that hatched during the spill had open sores, so they could not be sold for food.

To help the herring population recover, fishing was banned for a year and limited for several more years by the Alaska Department of Fish and Game. That strategy worked for the fish, but it was hard for people who depended on fishing for their living. Some could not afford to keep their fishing boats. A number of people who worked in fish processing plants moved away and took other jobs.

Weakened by the oil spill, much of the herring population suffered from a virus that attacks weak fish. The virus causes open sores like the ones on the affected fish at the top of the photograph.

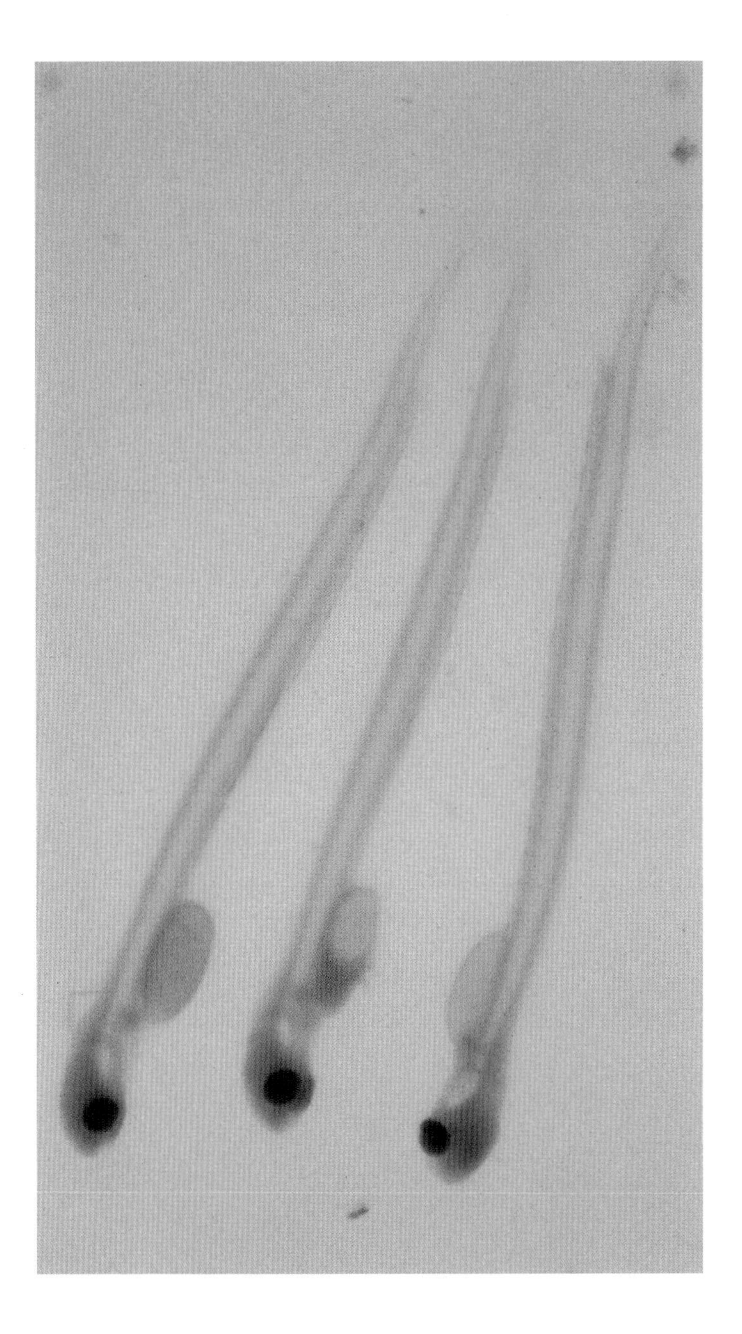

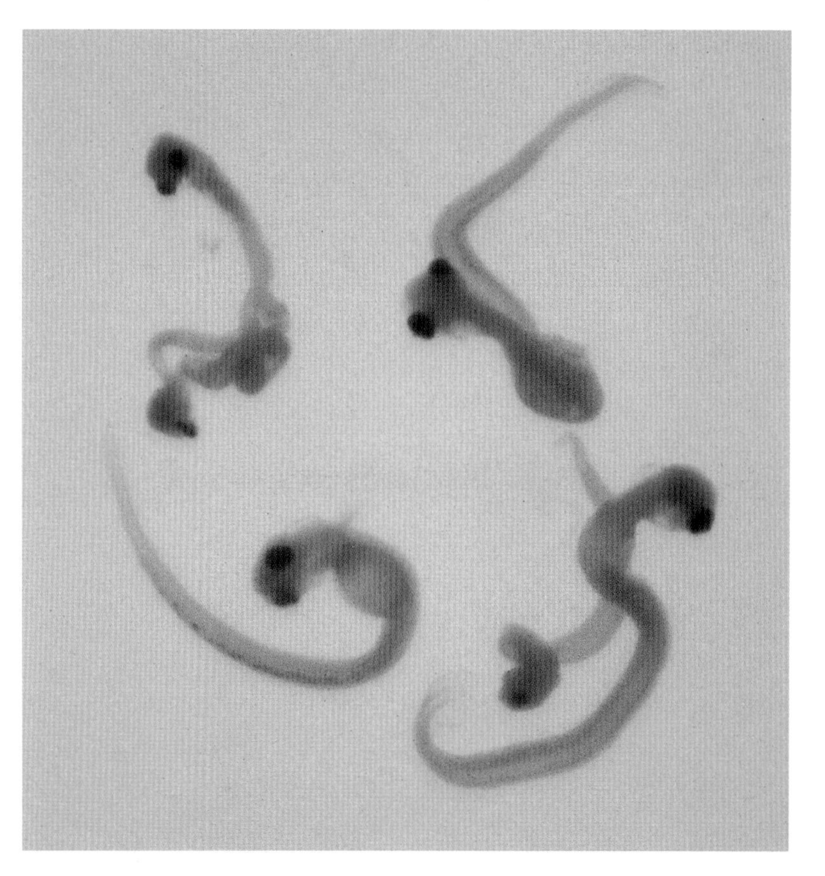

Many of the herring that hatched in the oil-polluted water were deformed. These photographs show healthy, normal herring (left) and deformed herring larvae (above).

Did the Oil Spill Affect People Too?

One place especially affected by the oil spill was Chenega, a small village on the edge of Prince William Sound.

The residents of Chenega are mainly Native Americans who, like their grandparents and great-grandparents, have always depended on Prince William Sound for food. Living much the way their ancestors did, the Chenega residents collected mussels on the beach and caught fish and seals.

When the black oil sloshed ashore on Chenega's beach, this community changed forever.

This is a view of Chenega. This wasn't the first time Chenega faced disaster. In 1964 an earthquake destroyed the village and residents had to rebuild.

After the spill, the people of Chenega were afraid to eat anything that came from the Sound. Scientists reported that any fish or seals that survived the spill were safe to eat, but the people of Chenega did not believe the reports. Without the natural resources of the Sound, Chenega residents were forced to take drastic action to feed their families.

Many left Chenega to find jobs. They worked on the oil cleanup teams or in the town of Valdez. With the money they earned, they bought food and hired a plane to fly the supplies to Chenega. Later, when the crisis was over, some people decided they liked living in a more modern town. Because they never returned, the population of Chenega is now only about half the size it was before the spill.

A boom, a floating fence, was supposed to trap oil washed off the Chenega shore so it could be skimmed up. However, tides repeatedly pushed under the fence and washed the oil back onto the shore before it could be collected. Then the beach had to be sprayed clean again.

The spill also changed Valdez, even though it was not directly affected by the oil. Because the town was the center of the cleanup operation, its population exploded within weeks after the spill, going from 3,500 to over 13,000 people. Imagine having the population of your town grow to more than three times its size in just a few weeks!

Most of the new people in town were cleanup workers. There were also Exxon officials, scientists, volunteers to help the animals, and newspaper and television reporters from around the world. The few hotels in town were quickly filled. Soon every family with an empty bedroom was renting to a stranger, and vacant lots were filled with tents.

Before the spill, most of the boats in this harbor would have been fishing boats. During the cleanup, every available boat in the harbor was hired by Exxon. Now many are tour boats.

The Keystone Hotel (inset) has a special connection to the spill. It was originally built by Exxon and served as its headquarters during the cleanup operation (shown above). After the cleanup, bathrooms were added to the offices to transform the building into a hotel.

Just after the spill, cars and boats were even harder to find than beds. There were no rental cars in town, so for a while, some families earned extra money by renting their cars. Later, to fill the huge demand, cars arrived by the truckload.

It was a boost to the economy to have so many people in Valdez, but it was also hard for such a small town to support so many people. Trucks loaded with food had to be hauled into town to feed everyone. There were also increased demands for basic services such as electricity, water, and sewage treatment.

The cleanup lasted a very long time—mainly from 1989 through 1992. In some places, the cleanup effort is still going on. In others, the beaches are back to normal.

What Is Being Done to Prevent Future Spills?

As a result of the *Exxon Valdez* oil spill, Congress passed the Oil Pollution Act in 1990 to help prevent future accidents. Today, oil tankers are stronger, and there are more safeguards against spills.

The SERVS (Ship Escort & Response Vessel Service) vessel is especially equipped to handle cleanup operations. Under what looks like two orange domes (right) on the rear deck are big hoses designed to suck oil off the surface of the water.

SERVS also maintains cleanup barges at several locations in the Sound. Because precious time could be wasted transporting crews to remote locations in the Sound, workers take turns waiting close to places where ships could get into trouble and possibly cause an oil spill.

In the event of a future oil spill, the crew of a SERVS vessel would start cleanup immediately. In case of a leak while a tanker is being filled, a containment boom surrounds the ship (bottom left).

Extra care is taken to make sure oil and the water in Prince William Sound don't mix in the future. Nearly 1,000 of the people in Valdez work for the Coast Guard or Aleyska, guarding against spills or ready to launch a quick cleanup.

To make sure ships don't have trouble while they are crossing the Sound, tankers are required to maintain speed limits and to stay within shipping lanes. Two tugboats also escort each tanker. That way, if the tanker should lose power, it won't drift onto the rocks. The twin tugboats can keep even a huge, fully loaded oil tanker in place until the problem is solved.

Since the spill, extra care has also been taken to keep any oil from seeping into Prince William Sound. In case of an emergency, a large part of the fishing fleet has received training on how to quickly contain and clean up spilled oil.

To make sure every tanker stays safely away from Bligh Reef where the Exxon Valdez *ran aground, the rocks are now marked with a lighted beacon. Buoys define the sea lane.*

What Is Prince William Sound Like Today?

The oil spill also changed Valdez by making it world famous. Tourists flock to the area every summer to see this special place they discovered on the news. Before the spill, Valdez only had 20 bed-and-breakfasts. During the cleanup operation, that number exploded to 150, and today there are still about 100—proof of a strong tourist business.

Large areas of land and portions of the Sound have been closed to commercial fishing and land development. Protecting these areas helps animal populations recover. At the same time, it also serves as a way to attract tourists. An abundance of campsites, trails, and docks enable people to enjoy this beautiful area.

In the summer, it's daylight in Valdez nearly twenty-four hours a day, so tourists have plenty of time to enjoy the area's many activities.

How Are the Animals Today?

What about the animals that live in or around Prince William Sound? Have they recovered from the oil spill? The answer depends on the kind of animal.

It's uncertain whether the sea otter population will recover from the spill, but success depends in part on the recovery of their habitat. For sea otters to do well, the populations of the fish, crabs, and snails that they eat must recover too. The key is the recovery of brown seaweed in the area just offshore. The large leaves of the adult plants are home to snails and limpets and shelter young fish. Besides being oiled, the brown seaweed was killed by the high-pressure, hot-water wash used to clean the beaches. This just goes to show that anything that disrupts an environment hurts the whole web of life living there.

The sea otter's survival is tied to the recovery of brown seaweed, which houses the snails and crabs that the otters eat.

The bald eagle population was the first to rebound. The year after the spill, it was already on the rise. By 1997, it was the only population to be listed as fully recovered by the *Exxon Valdez* Oil Spill Trustee Council. After the spill, bald eagles that had been unable to find suitable nests took over the nests abandoned by birds that had died. The most recent survey taken in 1997 counted about 5,000 bald eagles living around the Sound—1,000 more than before the spill.

Prince William Sound is once again a good place for eagles to fish.

The oil spill hurt some animals that were already in trouble. For example, the harbor seal population was already low. Then hundreds of seals died because of the spill. Rather than recovering, the seal population has continued to shrink. Researchers are trying to understand why this decline is occurring. Because harbor seals travel long distances to hunt for fish, researchers are using monitoring devices and satellites to track the seals and may soon know exactly where they go to find food.

Other animal populations, including cormorants and pigeon guillemots, have also decreased. No one is quite sure why this is the case or if these animal populations will rebound in the future. Everyone knows for sure that future oil spills must be prevented if these animals are to survive.

Many harbor seal pups died after being born on oily beaches.

Is the Oily Mess Completely Cleaned Up?

What about the community of Chenega? It's still struggling to recover. Even the effort to clean up its beach continues. So much oil washed ashore that despite repeated cleanup efforts, oil continues to seep out of the sand beneath the rocks.

It may take many more years, but eventually the weather and the waves will clean away all traces of the *Exxon Valdez* oil spill from the beaches of Prince William Sound—even from Chenega. The emotional impact of the spill, though, can't be corrected by the forces of nature. Those changes are likely to have an effect—for better or worse—that lasts forever.

Larry Evanoff sits on the beach at Chenega in the summer of 1997—eight years after the spill. He is holding a tarry ball of weathered oil that was just removed from the beach.

Glossary/Index

Aleyska: The company that runs the Trans-Alaska Pipeline and loads the oil into tankers in Port Valdez. From there, the oil is transported to refineries. 5, 19

Animal Cleaning: Volunteers worked together to clean up oiled animals—a process that was very stressful for the animals. 6–9

Bald Eagle: This predatory bird has a large head, a short tail, and a wing span as great as 200 centimeters (80 inches). Young eagles have brown heads until they are about four years old. Mature adults have white heads. 24–25

Bligh Reef: A jumble of rocks that makes the Sound shallow—too shallow for a big tanker to cross safely. 4, 18

Chenega: A small village on an island in Prince William Sound that relies on fishing and seal hunting to support its economy. During the 1964 Alaska earthquake, the town was badly damaged and had to be rebuilt. 14–17, 28, 29

Containment Boom: A floating barrier used to trap oil on the surface of the water. 16, 19

Exxon: A large oil company that owns the *Exxon Valdez* and many other oil tankers. 5, 9, 19

***Exxon Valdez*:** The oil supertanker that caused the spill. After the spill, it was repaired but banned from Port Valdez. Renamed the *SeaRiver Mediterranean*, the ship continues to transport oil through the Mediterranean and up to northern Europe. 2–4, 21

Harbor Seal: A small marine mammal. Both males and females may grow to be as long as 2 meters (about 6 feet) and weigh over 136 kilograms (300 pounds). Their coloring varies from silver to black, but the most common is light gray with dark spots. 26–27

Herring: A large cold-water fish that is blue-green on top and silver along its sides. Herring are covered with large scales and may grow up to 45 centimeters (18 inches) in length. 12–13

Oil Slick: A layer of oil on the surface of the water. 4

Pigeon Guillemot: A small black bird with white markings on its wings. It eats fish in shallow waters near the shoreline of the Sound. 6, 7

Pink Salmon: One of the many breeds of salmon, the pink salmon is a blue-hued fish with pink flesh. It can grow up to 62 centimeters (about 25 inches) in length. Just before spawning, males turn black with white bellies and females become olive green with lighter green bellies. 10–11

Prince William Sound: An inlet of the Gulf of Alaska. Many animals use the Sound as a nursery for their young. 3–5, 18–19, 22–23, 28–29

Sea Otter: A furry marine mammal that is at home in the cold Alaskan water. It lacks a layer of fat to insulate it from the cold water, but has thick fur to keep it warm. 8–9, 22–23

Sockeye Salmon: This grayish silver fish changes to a deep red when it is ready to reproduce. The adults grow to be over 50 centimeters (20 inches) long and weigh as much as 3 kilograms (about 6 pounds). 11

SERVS: This is the Ship Escort & Response Vessel Service. It is charged with the job of preventing future oil spills in Prince William Sound and Valdez. 18

Valdez: A town that serves as both a fishing harbor and the shipping point for oil from Alaska. 18–19

For the children of Chenega.

The author thanks the following individuals for sharing their enthusiasm and expertise: Dr. Alan Mearns, leader, BioAssessment team, Hazardous Materials Response and Assessment Division, NOAA; Deborah Payton, oceanographer, Modeling and Simulation Studies team of NOAA/ HAZMAT; John Wilcock, fishery research biologist, Alaska Department of Fish and Game; and Dr. Kathy Frost, biologist, Alaska Department of Fish and Game.

First published in the United States of America in 1999 by Walker Publishing Company, Inc.

Published simultaneously in Canada by Fitzhenry and Whiteside, Markham, Ontario L3R 4T8

Library of Congress Cataloging-in-Publication Data
Markle, Sandra.
After the spill: the *Exxon Valdez* disaster, then and now/Sandra Markle.
p. cm.
Summary: Examines the impact of the 1989 *Exxon Valdez* oil spill on the environment and people of Prince William Sound and describes the steps taken to minimize the damage and prevent a recurrence.
ISBN 0-8027-8610-3 (hc.) —ISBN 0-8027-8611-1 (rein.)
1. Oil spills—Environmental aspects—Alaska—Prince William Sound Region—Juvenile literature. 2. Tankers—Accidents—Environmental aspects—Alaska—Prince William Sound Region—Juvenile literature. 3. *Exxon Valdez* (Ship)—Juvenile literature. [1. Oil spills—Alaska—Prince William Sound Region. 2. Tankers—Accidents. 3. *Exxon Valdez* (Ship)] I. Title.
TD427.P4M377 1999
363.738'2'097983—dc21 98-38550
CIP
AC

Photo Credits: Larry Evanoff: 14; Exxon: 19, 20; Kathy Frost: 28; Greenpeace: 6; Rich Kirchner: 8, 10, 24, 26; Jim Lavrakas, *Anchorage Daily News*: 29; Sandra Markle: 1, 16, 18, 19, 21, 22, 23, 31; Oil Spill Public Information Center: 16; Chris Rose, U. S. Coast Guard: 2, 3; John Wilcock, Alaska Department of Fish and Game: 12, 13.

Map on page 4 © Joe LeMonnier

The front jacket photograph, by Kathy Frost, was taken two months after the spill; the title page photograph (also on page 22), by Sandra Markle, depicts the area after the completion of the cleanup.

Book design by Maura Fadden Rosenthal/Mspace

Printed in Hong Kong

10 9 8 7 6 5 4 3 2 1